Teach Me How To Swaddle

Four Easy Steps

Author and Illustrator

Kimberly C. Townsend

DEDICATION

I dedicate this book to my wonderful son.
He is a very happy baby. I am writing these books to help other parents
have a wonderful experience raising their children.
Everyday is a special day.
Remember, you can never get today back,
so make the best of each new day.

CONTENTS

ACKNOWLEDGMENT

I would like to acknowledge my parents.
Thank you for your support and constant encouragement.
You have always put your children first and sacrificed so much.
I thank you both for all you have done for me and my son.

Teach Me How To Swaddle

STEP ONE

Start with a blanket, turned in a diamond shape.

Place baby in the upper center of the blanket.

Optional: fold top corner behind baby's shoulders.

STEP TWO

Place the baby's right arm to the side and take that corner across the body and tuck it under the baby on the opposite side.

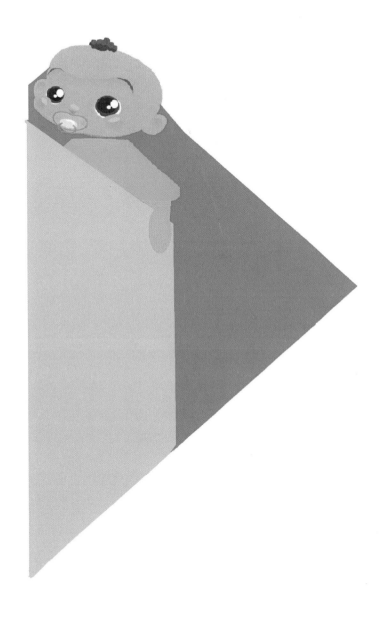

Optional: a blanket with some stretch helps.

STEP THREE

Take the bottom corner over the baby's body and tuck it behind the baby's left shoulder.

Special Note: Make sure the blanket is secure but not tight. You **do not** want the swaddle to be so tight that it prevents the lungs from expanding. Slight movement is encouraged for healthy growth. Always watch your child to make sure nothing is prohibiting breathing and blocking air passages.

STEP FOUR

Place the other arm down by the side and take that corner around the baby's body and tuck it in the upper center.

YOU DID IT!

If you're ever in doubt practice on a doll or stuff animal.
Practice makes perfect.
Swaddling helped comfort my baby.
The baby is used to being in a warm confined space.
I noticed when my baby was a newborn he was a little jumpy.
This was mainly caused by a new environment; just the extra stretch of his limbs can be alarming.
The swaddling technique was helpful to me and my newborn, and I hope it also works just as well for you.

Please visit

www.babygibberish.com

Made in the USA
Las Vegas, NV
23 April 2023